501

SECRETS TO SUCCESSFUL

SELLING

CARLTON MASI

MASI MOTIVATIONAL COMPANY

501 Secrets To Successful Selling

BY CARLTON MASI

Published by: Masi Motivational Company
22020 Clarendon Street, Suite #103
Woodland Hills, California 91367
Phone • (800) 800-9736
Fax • (800) 800-9735
Web Site • www.MasiTrains.com

About the Author
CARLTON MASI

Currently featuring his powerful "Selling With Passion", "Customer Service Champions", "Leading Sales Superstars", and "Soaring To Success" training seminars, the president of Masi Motivational Company has created a new vision for those seeking to advance their personal careers.

Now the country's foremost motivational speaker in sales and customer service training, Carlton will teach you how to take advantage of the trends which are reshaping consumer buying decisions.

Carlton believes that decision makers today have less time, more responsibility, and more stress than ever before. Managers are being pushed to streamline, reduce costs, and cut overhead. This paradox creates unprecedented opportunities. However, old school techniques don't work in reaching today's marketplace. Today, corporations are looking for new solutions which can make them more successful. This book will provide you with some new ideas and motivation to exceed your customers' expectations!

Acknowledgments

Words could not possibly express my love,
friendship, and appreciation.

Trinda and Harry Masi
Christine and Joseph Suzuki
Irwin Lieberman
Liza Polin - Shaun Martin
Tico

Special thanks to Angie Schiffner
who has been the inspiration and true champion
of Masi Motivational Company.

SECRET NO. 1

Be proud of your profession.
Without salespeople,
the world would stand still.

SECRET NO. 2

Be reading a new sales
book all the time.

🐦 SECRET NO. 3

Buy a new tie at Nordstrom once a month.

🐦 SECRET NO. 4

Make at least 14 cold calls per day either by phone or in person.

ॐ SECRET NO. 5

Always use a "nice" pen.

ॐ SECRET NO. 6

Get proficient with Contact Management Software.

❧ SECRET NO. 7

Begin your day selling before others begin their day selling.

❧ SECRET NO. 8

Never stop prospecting.

🐚 SECRET NO. 9

Believe 100% in your product / service.

🐚 SECRET NO. 10

Always carry an extra pair of contact lenses.

❧ SECRET NO.11

Take night flights whenever possible so that you can sell during the day.

❧ SECRET NO.12

Applaud favorites but always root for the underdog.

❧ SECRET NO. 13

Only 14% of salespeople ask for the order until they get it. Never stop asking.

❧ SECRET NO. 14

Never sit down in the reception area when waiting for a prospect or customer. Initial body positioning is important to starting a call off right.

ಮ SECRET NO.15

Know all the features and benefits of your products and services.

ಮ SECRET NO.16

Continuously inform inside support people on target accounts which may order soon.

❧ SECRET NO. 17

Never drink alcohol at lunch.

❧ SECRET NO. 18

After answering a question, always ask a question so that you stay in control of the conversation.

৶ SECRET NO. 19

Sing in the shower.
It will make you happy
for your first call.

৶ SECRET NO. 20

Never ask a prospect or
customer to "sign" anything.
Instead, use one of these options:
approve, acknowledge,
authorize, or OK.

❧ SECRET NO. 21

Decide in advance to win all sales contests.

❧ SECRET NO. 22

Receptionists are brilliant. Treat them as professionals and they will help you accomplish your goal.

❧ SECRET NO. 23

Don't wear too much make-up or jewelry.

❧ SECRET NO. 24

When you want someone to say "yes", let them see "yes" by nodding. Our mind reacts 85% of the time to visual stimulation.

❧ SECRET NO. 25

Add something new to your sales tool box every month.

❧ SECRET NO. 26

Always keep a note pad and pen by your bedside. You'll be amazed at the creative ideas you come up with during the middle of the night.

❦ SECRET NO. 27

Upgrade your presentation at least once a quarter. It will keep you ahead of the competition.

❦ SECRET NO. 28

Don't be disappointed if a prospect cancels at the last minute. Use the "guilt factor" to your advantage – reschedule immediately.

੨ SECRET NO. 29

Customers have a choice. They can buy from you, they can buy from someone else, or they can buy from no one. Your expertise will decide their fate.

੨ SECRET NO. 30

Quality and price are never the primary reason for buying anything. Both of these are based on logic and people don't buy logically – they buy emotionally.

SECRET NO. 31

Wear a nice watch.

SECRET NO. 32

Become obsessed about providing superior customer service.

❧ SECRET NO. 33

List your top five competitors. What is their edge?

❧ BONUS SECRET ❧

Be careful of commission only compensation plans.

ॐ SECRET No. 34

Keep lots of change in the ashtray of your car. You'll need it for the meter.

ॐ SECRET No. 35

When cold-calling office buildings, walk deliberately towards the elevators. Security personnel don't usually stop people who know where they are going.

❧ SECRET NO. 36

Learn how to send a "broadcast fax".

❧ SECRET NO. 37

Send cards regularly.

❦ SECRET No. 38

You will sell more when your self-confidence and self-esteem are at their highest.

❦ SECRET No. 39

Become great at remembering names. When introduced to someone, always concentrate on their name and repeat it back to them twice if possible.

ℰ❧ SECRET No. 40

You must have a cellular phone, but be smart with it – it's overhead.

ℰ❧ SECRET No. 41

Planned presentations are always more effective.

❧ SECRET NO. 42

If you're not out selling, you're being outsold.

❧ SECRET NO. 43

You don't have to become friends with the prospect before they will buy, but you must gain their respect and trust before they will give you their money.

❧ Secret No. 44

If it's to be, it's up to me.

❧ Secret No. 45

Winners use time while losers get used by time.

❧ SECRET NO. 46

Don't worry about "No Soliciting" signs. Those inside forget the signs are even there.

❧ SECRET NO. 47

80% of all sales are made after the 5th call. Get excited when the prospect says "no"! You're that much closer to a sale.

❧ SECRET NO. 48

Know your distinct "competitive edge".

❧ SECRET NO. 49

Limit your active data-base to 180 clients and prospects. When the universe gets too big, you become less effective.

❧ SECRET NO. 50

Eliminate negative self-talk.

❧ SECRET NO. 51

When beginning your presentation, always remind the prospect of the purpose of your call. Your opening line should significantly pique their curiosity.

ಏ BONUS SECRET ৯৯

Consider dry cleaning an investment. Your customers can tell the difference.

ಏ SECRET NO. 52

62% of all your customers will consider making a change to another vendor over the next 6 months. What action steps have you taken to insure that they will remain your customers?

☙ SECRET NO. 53

Keep extra batteries for your pager.

☙ SECRET NO. 54

Wear nametags on the right so that people can (more easily) see your name when shaking your hand.

☙ SECRET NO.55

Carry lots of business cards.

☙ SECRET NO.56

Rent expensive cars for pleasure, not for business.

ॐ SECRET NO. 57

Attend sales seminars.

ॐ SECRET NO. 58

Enthusiasm is contagious,
bring it back to the office
and share it.

❧ SECRET No. 59

Eliminate sales call reports, put your time into Strategic Action Plans instead.

❧ SECRET No. 60

Only the lead dog gets a change of scenery.

❧ SECRET No.61

Don't bite your nails.

❧ SECRET No.62

Encourage your prospect to talk about the problems they have had or anticipate having so they'll be emotionally involved in the conversation.

৵ SECRET NO. 63

*Big billers are as good
on the phone as they
are on their feet.*

৵ SECRET NO. 64

*What we sell and what
the buyer buys are not always
the same thing.*

🐚 SECRET NO.65

See your dentist frequently.

🐚 SECRET NO.66

Avoid promising too much too quickly.

❧ SECRET NO. 67

Before you go home, prepare the next day's calls in advance.

❧ SECRET NO. 68

Forget rejection. You didn't have anything before you made the call. After all, what's less than zero?

❧ SECRET NO. 69

Keep activity goals and results desired in the proper perspective.

❧ SECRET NO. 70

Become masterful at using open ended questions. You will be pleasantly surprised with how far you can get with Who, What, When, Where, Why and How!

❧ SECRET NO. 71

Have a dog or cat. They are great listeners and would love to hear your "first time" presentations.

❧ SECRET NO. 72

Know how to answer the typical objections before you get them.

❧ SECRET NO. 73

Be determined to have an "action" come out of every call.

❧ SECRET NO. 74

Smile.

❧ SECRET NO.75

Buy a notebook computer.

❧ SECRET NO.76

Don't stop making calls once you start.

❧ SECRET NO. 77

Concentrate on your delivery. It will help your audience stay interested.

❧ SECRET NO. 78

Use quality marketing materials.

SECRET No. 79

If you visualize the prospect coming out to see you – they will more often.

SECRET No. 80

Fear of failure doesn't exist if you believe it doesn't.

☙ SECRET NO. 81

Achieve balance in your life. Spend more time with your family.

☙ SECRET NO. 82

Learn the importance behind "mirroring and matching" prospect body language.

ê SECRET NO. 83

Persistence will whip fears and rejection.

ê SECRET NO. 84

Buy flowers for yourself someday.

ॐ SECRET NO. 85

Practice the "golden sales rule": Sell to others as you would want them to sell to you.

ॐ SECRET NO. 86

Project a "consultative selling" demeanor.

❧ SECRET NO. 87

Never stay at a client's too long.

❧ SECRET NO. 88

Face your prospect, lean forward and listen attentively without interruption.

SECRET NO. 89

Question for clarification. Say, "How do you mean?"

SECRET NO. 90

When you walk into a prospect's office to begin a presentation, begin speaking before you sit. This will help you avoid the initial "pressure of the silence."

❧ SECRET NO.91

Don't be thinking of your next question too soon.

❧ SECRET NO.92

Be completely prepared before you go into a presentation.

❧ SECRET No. 93

Involve the prospect early in the presentation in order to capture interest.

❧ SECRET No. 94

Wash your hands after pumping gas.

☙ SECRET NO. 95

Sell to help, not for commissions. You'll make more money.

☙ SECRET NO. 96

Watch the movie "Glengarry GlenRoss" in order to learn what not to do.

❧ SECRET NO.97

You can achieve anything for which you are willing to pay the price.

❧ SECRET NO.98

The competition thins out at the top.

SECRET NO. 99

The marketplace thrives on "something new" every 21 days, so give them something new.

SECRET NO. 100

Corporations don't pay your compensation.
Customers pay your compensation.
Get more customers.

❧ SECRET No. 101

Pull your socks up from the bottom.

❧ SECRET No. 102

There are two main buying motivators: The Hope of Gain and The Fear of Loss. Use them to your advantage.

ଛ SECRET NO. 103

Brainstorm often.

ଛ SECRET NO. 104

You work for yourself. When you think you work for someone else, you're lagging behind those that see themselves as owners of their own companies.

SECRET No. 105

Simplify, but intensify your goals.

SECRET No. 106

Surprise your customers on their birthday.

❧ SECRET NO. 107

Emphasize service after the sale.

❧ SECRET NO. 108

Don't shy away from the biggest and most affluent prospects. Remember, they are people too.

❧ SECRET NO. 109

Have a printed customer list with you at all times.

❧ SECRET NO. 110

Tell your prospects stories of how you helped another customer who had similar challenges.

❧ Secret No. 111

You should consider yourself an asset, not a nuisance when calling on prospects.

❧ Secret No. 112

Get rid of prospects who don't belong in your database. Ask yourself, "Why does this company deserve to have me calling on them?"

ॐ SECRET NO. 113

You are only selling when you are "face-to-face" with a real live prospect.

ॐ SECRET NO. 114

Use color copied testimonial letters.

ॐ SECRET No. 115

Drop names of larger customers or the buyer's competitors when appropriate.

ॐ SECRET No. 116

When on the road, call home every night.

❧ SECRET NO. 117

Make fast food a last choice.

❧ SECRET NO. 118

Take prospects and customers to work-out, play golf, tennis, or other sports.

·❧ SECRET No. 119

Laugh lots. Have fun.

·❧ SECRET No. 120

Be the first to introduce yourself to your competition at trade shows.

ও SECRET NO. 121

Spend less time worrying.

ও SECRET NO. 122

Challenge yourself often to move outside your comfort zone.

SECRET NO. 123

Don't use the word "honestly" when selling to prospects.

SECRET NO. 124

After every call, ask yourself what you did right.

SECRET No. 125

All top salespeople are creative.

SECRET No. 126

Sell to every member of a decision-making committee.

ε❧ SECRET NO. 127

Cross-promote with other businesses when possible.

ε❧ SECRET NO. 128

Don't use the same solution to every challenge.

SECRET NO. 129

Provide request for information cards.

SECRET NO. 130

Send targeted direct mail to your prospects every 21 days.

SECRET NO. 131

Use coupon books or punch cards for repeat customers.

SECRET NO. 132

Watch the presentation style of newscasters. You can learn a lot.

❧ SECRET NO. 133

Know as much information about the prospect company before you meet with them.

❧ SECRET NO. 134

Create customer taped audio testimonials.

❧ SECRET NO. 135

When you meet with prospects, take great notes.

❧ SECRET NO. 136

Don't sell at lunch until the prospect asks.

ॐ SECRET No. 137

"Short Story" references make great drop-offs.

ॐ SECRET No. 138

Everyone's #1 job is selling.

ॐ SECRET NO. 139

Give service people the lead role in all immediate decisions.

ॐ SECRET NO. 140

Promote your extended hours.

ɜ SECRET NO. 141

When you goof, ask the magic question: "What can I do to make it right?"

ɜ SECRET NO. 142

Don't expect your customers to tell you they are unhappy with your level of service.

ё● SECRET No. 143

Customers like positive people.

SECRET No. 144
ё●

Celebrate when you make a big sale.

❧ SECRET NO. 145

Get up early and work late.

❧ SECRET NO. 146

Don't nickel and dime your clients.

❧ SECRET NO. 147

Set fees based on value, not time spent.

❧ SECRET NO. 148

Get something back when you give something away.

SECRET NO. 149

Know your limitations.
Avoid overcommitting.

SECRET NO. 150

Don't slack off after a big sale.
Turn it up another notch.

❧ SECRET No. 151

Monday mornings and Friday afternoons should be work time, not wasted time.

❧ SECRET No. 152

If you're losing money on a deal, you can never make it up on the volume.

ॐ SECRET NO. 153

Never assume anything when communicating with clients.

ॐ SECRET NO. 154

Admit when you are wrong.

 howe SECRET NO. 155

Today you must work harder and smarter.

howe SECRET NO. 156

Dedicate yourself to effective territory management.

❧ SECRET NO. 157

Use the word "investment" instead of "cost".

❧ SECRET NO. 158

Make that extra call at 4:45 p.m.

SECRET NO. 159

Proofread all correspondence.

SECRET NO. 160

Even when cold-calling from building to building, wear your seatbelt.

☙ SECRET NO. 161

Read the Sunday newspaper.

☙ SECRET NO. 162

Be nice to secretaries.

❧ SECRET NO. 163

Never say negative things about your company to your clients.

❧ SECRET NO. 164

Improve your speaking skills by enrolling in Toastmasters or by attending a Dale Carnegie course.

Secret No. 165

Make sure you always have a list of your prospects.

Secret No. 166

Always know what your customers have purchased in the past before you meet with them.

❧ SECRET No. 167

What other products or services do you have that will benefit your client?

❧ SECRET No. 168

What other departments could use your products or services?

⁊ SECRET NO. 169

Are your shoes polished?

⁊ SECRET NO. 170

Ask your client, "What do I need to do to insure that you will repeat your order with me?"

❧ SECRET NO. 171

Work from a neat desk,—it's easier to find the phone.

❧ SECRET NO. 172

How can I get the decision makers that are happy to introduce me and sell me to other decision makers?

ॐ SECRET No. 173

Men should have their ties tied before going into the office.

ॐ SECRET No. 174

You will not have food tomorrow if you put off hunting today. Keep cold calling.

ॐ SECRET NO. 175

Stay focused.

ॐ SECRET NO. 176

Give your business card to people you meet on the plane.

❧ SECRET NO. 177

Pause before replying and then answer thoughtfully.

❧ SECRET NO. 178

Begin every sales call by stating the purpose of the call in the words the buyer wants to hear.

❧ SECRET NO. 179

Avoid the phrases, "Yes, but . . .", and "Yes, however . . ."

❧ SECRET NO. 180

58% of those that say they are shopping around – aren't.

SECRET NO. 181

Never discuss price until the customer asks price.

SECRET NO. 182

Never discuss price without mentioning value and benefits at the same time.

❧ SECRET No. 183

Understand that whatever you charge, you'll always get resistance.

❧ SECRET No. 184

If you want a place in the sun, you've got to put up with a few blisters.

ॐ SECRET NO. 185

Men should wear expensive socks. They're noticed.

ॐ SECRET NO. 186

Arrive early at networking events. Hand pick the best prospects. Go get em! That's why you came.

‿ SECRET NO. 187

Send a fax to a prospect to remind them of certain special situations.

‿ SECRET NO. 188

Eliminate your rolodex. Use new scanning software to maintain and organize your business cards.

❧ SECRET NO. 189

Throw in some extras whenever possible.

❧ SECRET NO. 190

Automate whatever possible on-site for your customers. Technological linkages make it more difficult for them to change.

ᓚ SECRET No. 191

*Ask customers their opinion
on a potential new line
of business.*

ᓚ SECRET No. 192

*Send E-Mail. It's still fun
to have something waiting
in your personal mailbox.*

SECRET No. 193

Give customers useful promo items.

SECRET No. 194

Top salespeople don't just take orders — they create the need.

ello SECRET No. 195

Do the things that you fear and the death of fear is certain.

ello SECRET No. 196

Congratulate others in your organization when they make sales.

> SECRET No. 197

Follow-up every marketing letter with a call.

> SECRET No. 198

Design special reports for customers after the sale has been made.

❧ SECRET NO. 199

Make the first prospect meeting productive.

❧ SECRET NO. 200

Exhibit at trade shows.

🐌 SECRET NO. 201

Organize and participate in regular cold-call blitzes.

🐌 SECRET NO. 202

Send news releases to your clients and prospects.

SECRET NO. 203

Reward customers for referring new business your way.

SECRET NO. 204

Put all your clients and prospects on either a 7, 14, or 21 day call frequency.

❧ SECRET No. 205

Match persistence with moxie.

❧ SECRET No. 206

Begin at the beginning. What impression does the customer get in the first 60 seconds when walking into your office?

❧ SECRET NO. 207

Don't mail proposals.
Deliver them in person
whenever possible.

❧ SECRET NO. 208

Send your customers plants
or flowers on
special occasions.

SECRET No. 209

Don't plan when you could be selling.

SECRET No. 210

When you read an article that mentions a customer's name or contains useful information – clip it and send it with a note.

❧ SECRET NO. 211

Family should always come before sales.

❧ SECRET NO. 212

Select 25 key target accounts and put them on a 7 day call frequency for six weeks. You'll be amazed at what happens.

❧ SECRET NO. 213

Do it NOW!

❧ SECRET NO. 214

Breakfast appointments create sales opportunities.

৵ SECRET NO. 215

How much time do you spend a year drinking coffee? Low producers take coffee breaks.

৵ SECRET NO. 216

Celebrate the anniversary of when your customer became your customer.

✒ SECRET NO. 217

Five one-page brochures are better than one five-page brochure.

✒ SECRET NO. 218

Get a toll-free 800 number.

❧ SECRET NO. 219

Send out a regular newsletter.

❧ SECRET NO. 220

Give warranties and guarantees to reduce risk.

SECRET No. 221

Ask your customers for feedback – surveys.

SECRET No. 222

Customers buy more from salespeople they like.

ও SECRET NO. 223

Never use profanity in the presence of customers.

ও SECRET NO. 224

Find an eye-catching way to package your product.

♣ SECRET NO. 225

Make your signage sell.

♣ SECRET NO. 226

Handle complaints immediately.

ह्ब SECRET NO. 227

Underpromise, overdeliver.

ह्ब SECRET NO. 228

Do it right the first time.

ॐ SECRET NO. 229

Have more cash registers open than necessary.

ॐ SECRET NO. 230

Write thank-you notes for appointments, demonstrations, orders, and referrals.

 howl SECRET NO. 231

Expect to motivate yourself.

howl SECRET NO. 232

Always be on time
for appointments.

えか SECRET NO. 233

Listen to audio cassettes.

えか SECRET NO. 234

If you want to get to the top in your profession, sell to the top. It's always easier coming down than going up.

❧ SECRET NO. 235

Don't sell anything when you know there is something wrong.

❧ SECRET NO. 236

Ask yourself, "Is what I am doing right now leading to a sale?"

ॐ SECRET NO. 237

Get obsessed with "A" customers.

ॐ SECRET NO. 238

Respond promptly to all correspondence.

∂ SECRET NO. 239

Return phone calls right away.

∂ SECRET NO. 240

Listen to the customers you didn't get.

❧ SECRET No. 241

Make everything overly convenient for your customers.

❧ SECRET No. 242

Videotape yourself so you can see how you come across to customers.

❧ SECRET NO. 243

Have your car washed weekly.

❧ SECRET NO. 244

Accept full responsibility for your results.

દે SECRET NO. 245

If you don't love to sell,
get out of selling.

દે SECRET NO. 246

Be ethical.

❧ SECRET NO. 247

I've never seen a salesperson win an argument with a customer yet.

❧ SECRET NO. 248

Don't tell customers what they purchased before was wrong.

ॐ SECRET NO. 249

Keep up with world news.

ॐ SECRET NO. 250

Make 4 "Face-To-Face" client presentations per day with your first appointment at 9:00 a.m. every day.

ð SECRET NO. 251

Take the first step in sharing business leads. Most people will return the favor.

ð SECRET NO. 252

Don't lie on expense reports.

❧ SECRET NO. 253

Don't cheat on call reports.

❧ SECRET NO. 254

If you have to be the cheapest all the time, you need to learn more about sales.

❧ SECRET NO. 255

Become great at asking the closing question.

❧ SECRET NO. 256

38% of salespeople contact the buyer once and give up.

❧ SECRET NO. 257

Say nice things to your computer.

❧ SECRET NO. 258

Stop telling prospects you would "like to drop by because you'll be in the area." After all, why should <u>they</u> get together with you just because it is geographically convenient to <u>you</u>?

❧ SECRET NO. 259

Sales champions are awesome at follow-up.

❧ SECRET NO. 260

When leaving messages on voicemail, create some mystery. Don't give too much information.

₰ SECRET NO. 261

Eliminate buzzwords!
Your clients will find
it refreshing.

₰ SECRET NO. 262

Build telephone scripts
around spoken language
as opposed to
written language.

ॐ SECRET NO. 263

Good listening skills are critical.

ॐ SECRET NO. 264

When meeting with prospects, project a "consultative selling" demeanor.

❧ SECRET NO. 265

Emphasize service after the sale.

❧ SECRET NO. 266

Sell to help, not for commissions.

SECRET NO. 267

Don't be thinking of your next question too soon.

SECRET NO. 268

Make time to play.

❧ Secret No. 269

"House Accounts" will soon be buying from your competition.

❧ Secret No. 270

Get your hair cut often. It feels great.

ॐ SECRET NO. 271

Experienced salespeople can learn from new salespeople.

ॐ SECRET NO. 272

You get paid for results, not activity.

ℰ❧ SECRET NO. 273

Listening to the answer is far more important than ever asking the right question.

ℰ❧ SECRET NO. 274

The referral 3 step process: Describe the type of referral you want. Let them imagine faces. Ask directly and wait.

ᘒ SECRET NO. 275

Shake hands firmly.

ᘒ SECRET NO. 276

*When networking,
be aware of time. You must
meet other people.*

❧ SECRET NO. 277

It costs 5 times as much to get a new account as it does to keep the ones you already have.

❧ SECRET NO. 278

Keep updated street maps in your car.

❧ SECRET NO. 279

The quest for an edge over the competition should never cease.

❧ SECRET NO. 280

The call reluctant salesperson loses $10,800 per month in gross sales.

෧ SECRET NO. 281

Key Decision Makers are hard to get to, harder to meet, and easiest to sell.

෧ SECRET NO. 282

When you reach the Key Decision Maker by phone, your main objective is to set up an appointment.

❧ SECRET NO. 283

A lack of preparation is unprofessional and inexcusable.

❧ SECRET NO. 284

You have only 30 seconds at the beginning of the approach to get the person's complete attention.

ॐ SECRET No. 285

Three powerful influences are your appearance, voice, and attitude.

ॐ SECRET No. 286

Always try to minimize the noise and interruptions in the selling environment.

ஐ SECRET NO. 287

Nothing will kill a sale faster than a lack of enthusiasm.

ஐ SECRET NO. 288

Vision is the ability to see the invisible – it's healthy to dream about the future.

SECRET NO. 289

Wear comfortable shoes.

SECRET NO. 290

Thrive on making more money.

SECRET NO. 291

Incredible determination is a significant advantage.

SECRET NO. 292

Help prospects buy – don't sell them. You'll sell more.

❧ SECRET No. 293

Listen carefully when customers talk. They are giving you the golden key.

❧ SECRET No. 294

Give customers options on the best way to pay whenever possible.

❧ SECRET NO. 295

When creating action plans, set specific dates for accomplishment.

❧ SECRET NO. 296

Always call with valuable information. You will notice that your prospects are in fewer meetings if you do.

❧ SECRET NO. 297

Review your outcomes regularly.

❧ SECRET NO. 298

Always double check your credit card "available credit" before taking customers to lunch.

🐚 SECRET NO. 299

45% of salespeople ask for the order once and give up.

🐚 SECRET NO. 300

Always have a spare tire.

ଏଛ SECRET NO. 301

If you get a flat, call someone to fix it for you.

ଏଛ SECRET NO. 302

Project confidence.

❧ SECRET NO. 303

Be decisive.

❧ SECRET NO. 304

Running personal errands during the day shows a lack of commitment.

❧ SECRET No. 305

Make appointments at odd times. Avoid the hour and the half hour.

❧ SECRET No. 306

Unless buyers are talking about the problems they have had or anticipate having, they are not emotionally involved in the conversation.

ॐ SECRET No. 307

Sick days can be a real indicator of a sales slump.

ॐ SECRET No. 308

Whenever quoting a price, always ask two easy questions after stating the amount. You'll be amazed at how much less negotiating you do.

❧ SECRET NO. 309

Use visual sales aids when presenting. Show and tell works when we grow up too.

❧ SECRET NO. 310

Ask easy questions first – then progress to harder ones.

ๆ SECRET NO. 311

Show up often.

ๆ SECRET NO. 312

Continuously training yourself in all areas of interpersonal communication will be a big advantage.

SECRET No. 313

Before you can sell prospects, you must motivate, educate, and sell yourself.

SECRET No. 314

Your commitment is either increasing or decreasing relative to that of the competition.

❧ SECRET NO. 315

Never ask a question without having a good reason for asking.

❧ SECRET NO. 316

To be in the top 20%, you must have an insatiable hunger for victory.

❧ SECRET NO. 317

When you stop calling on customers, they stop buying from you.

❧ SECRET NO. 318

You are not selling when you are filling out forms or shuffling business cards.

❧ SECRET No. 319

Those who are not making a lot of money in selling are not talking to enough people.

❧ SECRET No. 320

Spend your entire day working – make every minute count.

❧ SECRET No. 321

Your car should be just as functional as your desk.

❧ SECRET No. 322

Master the approach close, the invitational close, the sudden-death close, the take-away close, the puppy dog close & the relevant story close.

ॐ SECRET No. 323

A referral is worth 10 to 15 times a cold call.

ॐ SECRET No. 324

Subscribe to selling magazines.

✍ SECRET No. 325

Offer a free gift when someone places their first order.

✍ SECRET No. 326

Drop off expensive pastries to a key prospect.

ଔ SECRET NO. 327

Have a "Private Preferred Customer" sale.

ଔ SECRET NO. 328

Give speeches to groups whose members are likely to need your services.

❧ SECRET NO. 329

Become active in your local chamber.

❧ SECRET NO. 330

Network with people from your church.

ॐ SECRET NO. 331

Write articles for trade magazines.

ॐ SECRET NO. 332

Start doing "small" things unannounced.

❧ SECRET NO. 333

Invite your prospects to an "in-house" luncheon. Let them tour your facilities.

❧ SECRET NO. 334

Give customers a financial incentive to order more.

SECRET NO. 335

Make sure customers can reach you 24 hours a day.

SECRET NO. 336

Be careful on how much you spend on yellow page ads. They are an <u>indirect</u> form of advertising.

SECRET NO. 337

Hustle often.

SECRET NO. 338

Be careful of the lead groups you join. Have a good idea in advance that they will pay off.

SECRET NO. 339

Prove to customers that the price is fair – not the cheapest.

SECRET NO. 340

Have a sales incubator board in your office . . . "Where customers are hatched." New ideas breed new customers.

❧ SECRET NO. 341

23% of salespeople contact buyers twice and give up.

❧ SECRET NO. 342

Park a little bit away from main entrances. Those inside don't need to be watching you as you get your things out of your car.

❧ SECRET NO. 343

*Never encourage the prospect
to brag about the competition.*

❧ SECRET NO. 344

*To reach the level of success
that most of us desire,
an edge is not a luxury,
it's a necessity.*

ॐ SECRET NO. 345

Receptionists are used to taking direction – so give them direction – politely.

ॐ SECRET NO. 346

Be determined to have an action come out of every call.

❧ SECRET NO. 347

Prospects will buy to solve a problem. Create solutions.

❧ SECRET NO. 348

When you get the Key Decision Maker on the phone, start slowly and speak with confidence.

SECRET No. 349

If you notice a prospect rubbing their chin, ask the closing question.

SECRET No. 350

The longer the question, the shorter the answer tends to be. The shorter the question, the longer the answer tends to be.

SECRET No. 351

If you attend a networking event with an associate – split up.

SECRET No. 352

Know how to handle these objections:

- We're happy with our current supplier.

- Send me some information.

- We're not looking at other services until . . .

❧ SECRET No. 353

Have your 30 second commercial down pat.

❧ SECRET No. 354

When you're demonstrating your products to prospects, let them touch and play too.

❧ SECRET NO. 355

Include a phone number on everything you distribute.

❧ SECRET NO. 356

When you get a referral, treat it like a million bucks – immediately!

❧ SECRET No. 357

Courage can take you to the top.

❧ SECRET No. 358

Keep a button repair kit on you. Be prepared to delegate if necessary.

❧ SECRET NO. 359

An extra pair of nylons in the glove compartment is not a bad idea.

❧ SECRET NO. 360

The less you carry, the less you drop.

🐌 SECRET No. 361

Prospects who have said "No" are good sources for referrals.

🐌 SECRET No. 362

Give prospects an opportunity to teach you something. It makes them feel great!

SECRET NO. 363

Keep spare keys hidden under your car.

SECRET NO. 364

Go cold calling in the rain. Your prospects will be impressed.

✒ SECRET NO. 365

Be careful with humor.

✒ SECRET NO. 366

Know when and when not to share personal life with your customers.

❧ SECRET No. 367

You should know exactly how much money you intend to earn in the next 12 months.

❧ SECRET No. 368

What part of the sales process are you weak at?

❧ SECRET NO. 369

Ask permission to ask questions before asking questions.

❧ SECRET NO. 370

Get gas the night before.

❧ SECRET No. 371

Presentations in lobbies usually don't go very well.

❧ SECRET No. 372

Be well prepared for sales meetings. Contribute more than your share, but don't steal the stage.

❧ SECRET No. 373

80% to 90% of your communication is nonverbal.

❧ SECRET No. 374

The planned presentation is much more powerful than the random presentation.

❧ SECRET NO. 375

Doing the right thing at the right time is more than luck.

❧ SECRET NO. 376

Plan your close in detail and then build your sales presentation on top of it.

SECRET No. 377

Refrain from discussions about religion and politics.

SECRET No. 378

Sometimes personalities between salespeople and prospects clash. When this happens, give the prospect to another salesperson. It's a good thing.

❧ SECRET NO. 379

There are no sales without objections.

❧ SECRET NO. 380

Don't blame others for not understanding your commission plan. It's your responsibility.

SECRET NO. 381

You have a choice everyday on the attitude that you will embrace for the day.

SECRET NO. 382

Success does not depend on a single sale.

&ℴ SECRET No. 383

Repeat business is earned and unearned.

&ℴ SECRET No. 384

Dare to be different.

❧ SECRET NO. 385

Know how much profit you are making on every order.

❧ SECRET NO. 386

Know how much commission you are earning on every order.

❧ SECRET No. 387

Purge your desk drawers at least once a quarter.

❧ SECRET No. 388

Put your name and address in the company database so you can see how your marketing materials make it through the mail.

❧ SECRET No. 389

Share your good ideas immediately with other sales people in your organization.

❧ SECRET No. 390

Never sidestep your credit department to make a sale.

ঌ SECRET NO. 391

Walk the walk.

ঌ SECRET NO. 392

Become a great hunter and the farm will always be there.

SECRET NO. 393

An adequate mix of prospects is the right recipe.

SECRET NO. 394

Too few appointments leads to not enough presentations which leads to not enough chances to close.

SECRET No. 395

Those who control the call, control the sale.

SECRET No. 396

Seek out your client's hot-button and keep pushing it over and over.

❧ SECRET No. 397

Don't try to convince when you should consult.

❧ SECRET No. 398

Be careful not to rush the sale. Remember, no wine is fine before its time.

⮿ SECRET NO. 399

Continuously restock your sales tool box with new items.

⮿ SECRET NO. 400

The "choice of words" you use will often make a difference.

ᒋᒧ SECRET NO. 401

Telephone equals money.

ᒋᒧ SECRET NO. 402

It's a numbers game, but don't spend too much time analyzing the numbers.

ᘓ SECRET NO. 403

Ask for bonuses after big sales.

ᘓ SECRET NO. 404

Would you hire you?

ॐ SECRET NO. 405

Be cautious about having too large a territory.

ॐ SECRET NO. 406

Sales meetings usually don't have enough "real world selling" situations in them.

❧ SECRET NO. 407

Discuss new methods of handling competition.

❧ SECRET NO. 408

Weekly sales statistics should be posted where everyone (except customers) can see them.

SECRET No. 409

Learn from lost sales.

SECRET No. 410

Be aware of television advertisements. You can learn a lot from somebody else's marketing budget.

❧ SECRET No. 411

Save mail you receive on new databases. You'll consider them someday.

❧ SECRET No. 412

Surprise ride-alongs by managers are a bad idea.

ॐ SECRET No. 413

Sales reps should not be using too much of their own money.

ॐ SECRET No. 414

Link rewards directly to performance.

SECRET No. 415

Contests lose steam when they are too long.

SECRET No. 416

Please and thank you go a long way.

* SECRET No. 417

Commission programs should never max out.

* SECRET No. 418

Little orders can someday turn into big orders.

❧ SECRET No. 419

Listen when you hear.

❧ SECRET No. 420

Have an open mind.
It works best in sales.

❧ SECRET NO. 421

Sales champions never have to lie about where they are going or where they have been.

❧ SECRET NO. 422

Your prospects and customers all hate being bored.

❧ SECRET NO. 423

Most brilliance comes from ordinary people working together in extraordinary ways.

❧ SECRET NO. 424

Avoid the phrase "You have such nice offices."

❧ SECRET NO. 425

The marketplace pays above average rewards for above average performance.

❧ SECRET NO. 426

25% of salespeople ask for the order twice and stop.

 how= SECRET NO. 427

Take vacations.

howi= SECRET NO. 428

Carry a small calculator all the time.

SECRET NO. 429

Avoid canceling appointments you make.

SECRET NO. 430

Unexpected bagels and cream cheese can go a long way.

🐌 Secret No. 431

It's fun to dance a little bit in the elevator after a good call.

🐌 Secret No. 432

A common mistake in many sales letters is an exaggeration of the benefits.

SECRET No. 433

Praise yourself often.

SECRET No. 434

Your need to sell and your prospect's need to buy are not always on the same schedule.

❧ SECRET No. 435

Get to bed before 11:00 p.m.

❧ SECRET No. 436

Being content as a "back-up vendor" reflects a complacent position.

❧ SECRET NO. 437

After you ask the closing question, remain silent!

❧ SECRET NO. 438

Present your business card from the corner so that your prospect can easily see your name.

❧ SECRET No. 439

Keep a hairbrush in the glove box for windy days.

❧ SECRET No. 440

Let your customers know how your organization is involved with charities.

❧ SECRET No. 441

Change your oil and rotate your tires often.

❧ SECRET No. 442

Make a list of all your friends. Who can they introduce you to?

❧ SECRET NO. 443

No guts, no glory!

❧ SECRET NO. 444

Follow the "25 Head Law". . . If there are 25 people or more in a room, I'm in there.

❧ SECRET No. 445

The less debt you have, the more you will sell.

❧ SECRET No. 446

At trade shows, you may have to play the role of the buyer before you get to be the seller.

ॐ SECRET No. 447

Find a way to meet Presidents and Owners.

ॐ SECRET No. 448

Remember, when customers whine, complain, and are difficult to service – they could be someone else's customer. Which would you prefer?

❧ SECRET NO. 449

When on sales calls, notice everything.

❧ SECRET NO. 450

Should you get down, just flap your wings faster – you'll be soaring again in no time.

ᔒ **SECRET NO. 451**

When you fall in love with the right person, sales increase.

ᔒ **SECRET NO. 452**

When touring a manufacturing facility, stop along the assembly line and ask questions. It will give your prospect a chance to brag.

❧ SECRET NO. 453

When you fall in love with the wrong person, sales decrease.

❧ SECRET NO. 454

Become conscious of remembering the details, they're so important.

❧ SECRET NO. 455

Never underestimate the future of a small business.

❧ SECRET NO. 456

Take pictures of your products as they are being assembled. Bring these to your prospects. You'll be amazed at the orders.

る **SECRET NO. 457**

Keep selling in December.

 る **SECRET NO. 458**

Suggest products of other vendors when you know they're a better solution. You will earn trust for the next opportunity.

SECRET NO. 459

Seek out your niche and attack.

SECRET NO. 460

Develop "How To" manuals and give them to your prospects before they buy.

🐦 SECRET NO. 461

Take computer training courses at night. They will pay off.

🐦 SECRET NO. 462

Make CFO's aware that you "might" be able to save the company money.

ࢠ SECRET NO. 463

The early bird gets the worm.

ࢠ SECRET NO. 464

Congratulate prospects and customers when you have learned of their new contracts.

❧ SECRET NO. 465

Using the phone on airplanes is too expensive.

❧ SECRET NO. 466

Use Avery labels-5160 for mass mailings. Delegate the affixing process.

ॐ SECRET No. 467

When your chin is down, you can't see the road ahead.

ॐ SECRET No. 468

Should a prospect decide to go with your competition, continue to follow-up. You will eventually get your shot if you stay the course.

🦢 SECRET NO. 469

Too much at lunch will slow your afternoon.

🦢 SECRET NO. 470

Refrain from selling accounts which would force you to make hasty hiring decisions.

❧ Secret No. 471

A well organized bedroom closet makes early mornings easier.

❧ Secret No. 472

If the fish smells bad, it probably is. Walk away from these potential accounts.

❦ SECRET No. 473

Seek out hotels which cater to the business traveler. You'll appreciate the extras.

❦ SECRET No. 474

Write hand written notes to prospects and customers. Watch your spelling and penmanship.

SECRET NO. 475

Even when you're comfortable with certain customers – don't use profanity.

SECRET NO. 476

Be careful of having too many "good conversations" with prospects – they may not be leading to sales.

SECRET No. 477

Back-up your database files often. Store disks off-site.

SECRET No. 478

When telephoning for appointments, always have a script, but never sound like you have one.

৯৯ SECRET NO. 479

The top pros practice all the time – role playing works!

৯৯ SECRET NO. 480

Read two books in the next six months on negotiating.

❧ Secret No. 481

Keep a small medical emergency kit in your car.

❧ Secret No. 482

When telephoning to get an appointment, use the phrase "When can we get together just briefly . . ."

❦ SECRET NO. 483

Avoid the phrases: I want to . . .
I need to . . . I'd like to . . .

❦ SECRET NO. 484

80% of salespeople make
20% of the sales.
20% of salespeople make
80% of the sales.

SECRET No. 485

Saturdays can be very productive work days.

SECRET No. 486

The marketplace pays below average rewards for below average performance.

SECRET NO. 487

Don't use your predecessor's poor notes as an excuse.

SECRET NO. 488

View all prospects as "key decision makers" until you find out differently.

❧ SECRET NO. 489

When cold calling, park your car in the shade whenever possible.

❧ SECRET NO. 490

Hand write "service call" notes the night before so that you don't have to waste time writing them in the car.

❧ SECRET NO. 491

If you're not <u>prospecting</u>, <u>presenting</u>, or <u>following-up</u>; you're wasting time.

❧ SECRET NO. 492

"Not a problem" is a key phrase which can comfort prospects concerns.

❧ SECRET NO. 493

"Unlike other services" is a powerful phrase when attempting to differentiate yourself from your competition.

❧ SECRET NO. 494

If you notice your proposal is not hitting the prospect's hot button, ask what they may consider as a "better alternative".

❧ SECRET NO. 495

Solutions which are suggested by prospects usually turn into sales for you!

❧ SECRET NO. 496

Calling into the office from your car several times a day is a waste of time. If it's important enough, the office will page you.

SECRET No. 497

When presenting in an office, be careful your eyes don't roam all over your prospect's desk.

SECRET No. 498

When out in the field, don't be so excited about "beating the traffic" back to the office. You're already in the best place!

SECRET No. 499

The things that we "Have-To-Do" can be very different from the things we "Choose-To-Do".

SECRET No. 500

A prospect's buying temperature always goes up when you get them to answer "yes" to your qualifying questions.

❧ SECRET No. 501

Make calls, make calls, make calls!

Notes

_____

_____

_____

_____

_____

_____

_____

_____

_____

_____

_____

_____

_____

_____

NOTES

_____

_____

_____

_____

_____

_____

_____

_____

_____

_____

_____

_____

_____

NOTES

_____

_____

_____

_____

_____

_____

_____

_____

_____

_____

_____

_____

_____

_____

_____

_____

NOTES

Notes

_____

_____

_____

_____

_____

_____

_____

_____

_____

_____

_____

_____

_____

_____

_____

NOTES